Data Management

*Almost "everything" you wanted to know
about data, but never dared to ask*

Fabrizio Zuccari

Cover by Davide Costamagna

Il potere dei dati sta nella loro capacità di rivelare verità nascoste. Ricorda: i dati possono anche mentire se non vengono interpretati correttamente.

The power of data lies in its ability to reveal hidden truths. Remember: data can also deceive if not interpreted correctly.

Content

Introduction

In recent years, the proliferation of digital devices, interconnected systems, and online platforms has led to an exponential growth in data generation. Organizations across every industry collect data from various sources, including customer interactions, sales transactions, social media, sensors, and IoT (*Internet of Things*) devices.

These data come in different forms, ranging from structured data such as databases and spreadsheets to unstructured data such as text, images, audio, and video. People themselves generate a significant amount of data through their online activities, such as browsing habits, social media posts, and mobile app usage. This personal data often contains sensitive information, such as financial details, health data, and personally identifiable information (PII).

With the increasing adoption of smart devices and the IoT, there is expected to be an exponential growth in data generation in the coming years. The growing volume and diversity of data present both opportunities and challenges.

On one hand, organizations can gain valuable insights, make data-driven decisions, and enhance customer experiences through advanced analytics and machine learning.
On the other hand, managing and protecting this vast and diverse landscape of data becomes complex.

Working in the IT field, increasingly in close contact with the business, and in a corporate environment where the roles of Business and IT are converging into a new professional figure, I wanted to write this essay with the idea of providing a basic understanding of many concepts and topics related to data, its actual value, and its management for those who do not have a "technical access" to this information but who, in modern companies, increasingly need to be able to effectively interact with more "technical" colleagues.

We will explore the concept of data, how its governance is structured, the key technologies, philosophies, risks, and complexities of management (both from a technical and legal perspective).

The hope is to provide a solid foundation for those who are less familiar with the subject to grow professionally.

What are Data?

Common technical terms:

1. ***Data***:
   Raw information or facts that represent an element of information.

2. ***Structured Data***:
   Data organized in a predefined format, such as tables in a database.

3. ***Unstructured Data***:
   Data without a specific format, such as free text, images, or videos.

4. ***Semi-Structured Data***:
   *Data that has partial structure, such as XML
   documents or JSON files.*

Regardless of the industry we operate in, data management
has become a key element for success and
competitiveness.
Whether it's companies seeking to better understand their
customers, researchers looking to uncover new insights, or
individuals wanting to make informed decisions,
understanding data and its implications is becoming
increasingly crucial.

But what exactly do we mean when we talk about "data"?

We will start by defining what data actually represents and
how it has become a fundamental element in our daily
lives.
We will then examine the different types of data that exist,
such as structured data, which follows an organized and
predefined schema; unstructured data, which lacks a
defined structure but contains a wide range of information;
and finally, semi-structured data, which presents an
intermediate level of organization.

Once we understand the nature of data, we will explore the
lifecycle that data goes through—from its acquisition,
through the stages of storage, processing, and analysis, to
its ultimate utilization. It will be important to understand
how data moves and transforms in its journey towards
value and usefulness.

Understanding what data are, the different types that exist,
and how they are managed in their lifecycle will lay the
foundation upon which to build a solid knowledge base in
the field of data management.

Data Definition

The term "data" refers to a symbolic representation of information that can be analyzed, interpreted, and used to make decisions.

Data can take various forms, such as text, numbers, images, or sounds.
EG: an email address, your bank account balance, or a photo taken with your smartphone are all examples of data.

Data has become extremely important in modern society for several reasons. Firstly, data allows us to gain valuable insights and knowledge. By analyzing data, we can identify patterns, trends, and correlations that help us make informed decisions.
EG: a company can use customer data to better understand their buying behaviors and adjust their marketing strategies accordingly.

Data has become a valuable resource for many organizations and businesses. It can be leveraged to gain competitive advantages, improve operational efficiency, and create new business opportunities.

Companies can use data to develop new products and services, identify new markets, or enhance internal processes.

Lastly, data also has a significant impact on our personal lives. We have virtual assistants that use data to answer our questions, personalized recommendations based on our interests, and artificial intelligence algorithms that assist us in decision-making.

Data Type: Structured, Unstructured and Semi-Structured

Data can be classified into different types based on its structure and organization.

Here are the three common types of data formats: *structured*, *unstructured*, and *semi-structured*.

- ***Structured Data***

  Structured data is organized in an orderly manner and follows a specific schema. It is presented in the form of tables or databases, where each field has a specific meaning.

  For example, imagine having a table to record personal information of individuals such as name, age, and address. Each row in this table represents a person, and each column represents a specific field like name, age, or address. This predefined schema makes it easy to organize and store data in an orderly fashion.

  Structured data can be managed using specific tools like spreadsheets or database software.
  These tools allow for easy and intuitive data entry, modification, and viewing.
  EG: using a spreadsheet like Microsoft Excel, you can create a table with desired fields and enter corresponding data in an organized manner.

  The structured nature of data also facilitates easy analysis.
  EG: you can use calculation functions to obtain the sum

of ages or count the number of people with a specific address.

This organized data structure simplifies processing and analysis using suitable tools.

* **_Unstructured Data_**

Unstructured data lacks a predefined structure. Unlike structured data, which is organized in tables or databases, unstructured data can take various types and formats.
This data can be textual, such as documents, emails, or social media posts, or it can be multimedia, such as images, videos, or audio files.

For instance, imagine having a collection of documents or emails. These data do not have a specific structure like tables but contain free-text information of various types.

Unstructured data often requires complex algorithms and advanced analysis techniques to extract meaningful insights.
EG: *if you have a large quantity of documents, you may use natural language processing algorithms to identify keywords, frequent phrases, or relationships between concepts.*

Additionally, if you have a collection of images, you may use computer vision algorithms to recognize objects or individuals within the images.

Despite the lack of a predefined structure, unstructured

data can contain a wealth of knowledge and valuable information. For example, social media posts can reveal user opinions on a specific topic, and images can provide visual details about events or locations.

When properly managed and analyzed, unstructured data can provide significant insights and support informed decision-making.

- *Semi-Structured Data*

Semi-structured data falls between structured and unstructured data.
This data exhibits some degree of structure but does not follow a rigid model like structured data.

example of semi-structured data is data in XML (*eXtensible Markup Language*) or JSON (*JavaScript Object Notation*) format: these formats allow for organizing data in a hierarchical structure while offering flexibility to represent information that may vary contextually.
EG: *an XML file representing book information may have tags like "title," "author," and "publication year" that follow a predefined structure. However, it may also have an optional tag like "description" that can vary from book to book. This means the presence of the "description" tag depends on the specific information associated with each book.*

Semi-structured data thus offers more flexibility than structured data, allowing for the management of information that can vary or be optional. However, unlike unstructured data, semi-structured data maintains a certain structure that facilitates understanding and processing.

When working with semi-structured data, specific tools can be used for processing and analysis. For example, you can use query languages like XPath to extract specific information from an XML document or utilize JSON libraries to manipulate data in JSON format.

Understanding these types of data is essential for data management as they require different approaches for organization, storage, and analysis.

Data Life Cycle

The data lifecycle represents the path that data follows from acquisition to utilization, including storage, processing, and analysis. Each phase is significant and contributes to value creation from data, enabling better understanding, decision support, and innovation.

The data **acquisition** phase involves collecting data from various sources, such as sensors, recording devices, online forms, or interactions with computer systems.
EG: *acquiring sales data from physical retail stores, browsing data from websites, or customer feedback data through online forms.*

Once acquired, data must be securely stored to enable long-term access and preservation. This can be done through the use of databases, physical storage systems, or cloud environments.

Subsequently, data can be **processed** to make it usable

and understandable. This may involve cleaning the data to remove errors or incomplete data, transforming formats to standardize the data structure, or applying algorithms to extract meaningful insights.

EG: processing sales data to calculate sales statistics or aggregating data to gain an overview of business performance.

Data **analysis** is a crucial phase where techniques and tools are applied to uncover patterns, trends, or relationships within the data. This allows for gaining insights and information that can guide informed decision-making and identify opportunities.

EG: identifying the most profitable customer segments or detecting anomalies in production data.

Finally, data are used to support decisions, generate reports, power artificial intelligence systems, or develop new solutions. The use of data can have a direct impact on decision-making processes and the outcomes of business or personal activities.

EG: using sales data to plan marketing strategies or an individual using fitness data to track their progress and adjust their training accordingly.

Metadata

Common technical terms:

1. ***Metadata***:
   Data that describes other data, such as attributes, structure, and data relationships.

2. ***Technical Metadata:***
   Information about the format, structure, and encoding of data.

3. ***Descriptive Metadata***:
   Information that provides details about the content and meaning of data.

4. ***Administrative Metadata:***
   Information about permissions, owners, and data management processes.

In the previous chapter, we explored the concept of data and its importance in modern society.

Now it's time to delve into a key element in data management: metadata.
The term "*metadata*" might sound complex, but it actually represents a fundamental concept for understanding and fully harnessing the potential of data.

Metadata and its role

Metadata are additional information that describes the data itself.
They are like "labels" that provide details about what the data is, how it is structured, and how it can be used. In books, metadata includes information such as the title, author, publication year, and genre. In digital files, metadata can contain information such as file size, format, creation date, and author.

Metadata plays a crucial role in data management because it allows for better organization, searchability, and understanding of information.
EG: *metadata can be used to classify and catalog data so that it is more easily discoverable and accessible.*

They can also help establish data access permissions, defining who can view or modify them.

Metadata can provide information about the context and quality of the data. For instance, metadata can indicate the data source, the method of collection, and the accuracy and reliability of the information.
This is particularly useful when conducting data analysis and interpretations, as metadata provides a basis for assessing the validity and suitability of data for a specific purpose.

They are extremely important for data sharing among different organizations or systems. They provide instructions on how to correctly interpret and use the data, avoiding ambiguity or interpretation errors.

Metadata Types

There are various types of metadata used in data management. Let's take a look at some of the most common ones:

Technical Metadata
Describes the technical characteristics of the data. This includes information such as file format, size, image resolution, or temporal data frequency. Technical metadata provides important technical details for data processing and manipulation, helping to ensure they are correctly interpreted and used.

Descriptive Metadata
Provides information about the content of the data. This can include textual descriptions, keywords, categories, or classifications that help better understand the meaning of the data. For example, an image can be described through descriptive metadata specifying the depicted object or the context in which it was taken. Descriptive metadata is particularly useful for data discovery and retrieval as it provides information that facilitates the discovery and access of relevant data.

Administrative Metadata
Relates to the management and administration of the data itself. This can include information such as data ownership, access policies, usage restrictions, and change history. Administrative metadata helps monitor and control data

access and usage, ensuring they are managed in compliance with regulations and company policies.

Structural Metadata

Describes the structure of the data and the relationships between elements. It is used to understand how data is organized and interconnected. In relational databases, structural metadata indicates tables, fields, primary and foreign keys used to define the database structure and relationships between tables.

Temporal Metadata

Provides information about the timing associated with the data. It can include the creation date, last modification date, and expiration date of the data. In email messages, temporal metadata can indicate when the message was sent, received, or modified.

Provenance Metadata

Tracks the origin and history of the data. It can include information such as the data source, the collection process, any transformations applied, and any modifications made. In weather data, provenance metadata can indicate the organization that collected the data, the instruments used to gather it, and the procedures followed to process it.

Metadata's Utility

Metadata is crucial for identifying, understanding, integrating, and protecting data. It plays a crucial role in their management and effective use by providing additional information that allows extracting the maximum value from the data itself.

Here are some of its main utilities:

Identification and Discovery:

Metadata is essential for identifying and finding relevant data. With information provided such as title, keywords, or classifications, it is possible to search and easily retrieve pertinent data within large quantities of information.
EG: when searching for a specific document in a vast collection of files, metadata like file name, author, or associated keywords can help locate it quickly and efficiently.

Interpretation and Understanding:

Metadata provides context and additional information that is essential for understanding the meaning and interpretation of data. Knowing the author, source, or creation date of data can influence its interpretation and reliability.
EG: in the case of a scientific article, metadata may indicate the name of the author researcher, institutional affiliation, and publication date. This information can help users evaluate the quality and reliability of the article.

Integration and Interoperability:

Metadata is essential for the integration and interoperability of data from different sources. By describing the data structure and relationships between them, metadata enables the harmonization and combination of different datasets.
EG: if you want to merge two databases containing similar information but with different schemas, metadata can provide guidance on how the data can be related and combined appropriately.

Security and Governance:

Administrative metadata is crucial for ensuring the security and integrity of data. By providing information about ownership, access, and restrictions, administrative metadata helps establish management policies and monitor the proper use of sensitive data.

EG: *administrative metadata can specify who has access and modification rights to the data, thus establishing appropriate control over the access and manipulation of sensitive information.*

Database

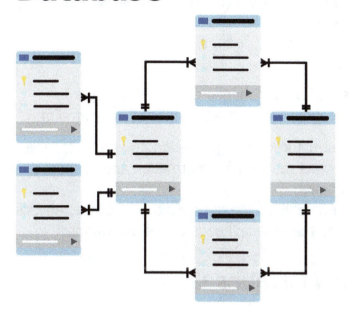

Common technical terms:

1. **Database:**
   An organized collection of structured and interconnected data, stored in a way that allows for efficient access and processing.

2. **Relational Database:**
   A type of database based on the relational model, where data is organized into tables with defined relationships between them.

3. **Unstructured Database:**
   A type of database where data does not follow a rigid schema and can be stored in various formats such as documents, images, or multimedia files.

4. ***Graph Database:***
   A type of database that uses graph structures to represent and store relationships between data, enabling complex queries based on node connections.

In the context of data management, databases play a fundamental role in data management and organization.

Through the structure and organization of data, databases allow us to extract meaningful information and support business decisions.
The choice of database type depends on the characteristics of the data and the specific needs of the application.

What is a database?

A database is a structured collection of data managed by a *DBMS* (***D**ata**B**ase **M**anagement **S**ystem*).

The DBMS allows for efficient and reliable organization, storage, retrieval, and management of data. Databases are widely used in various applications such as enterprise systems, websites, mobile apps, and much more.

The importance of databases in data management lies in their ability to provide a structured and consistent organization of data.
With a database, it is possible to define the data structure, establish relationships between them, and efficiently perform data querying and manipulation operations. This enables obtaining meaningful information from the data and supporting decision-making activities.

Database's Types

There are different types of databases, each designed to manage specific types of data and fulfill different needs.

The three main types of databases are:

- **Relational Database** (*RDBMS* **R**elational **D**ataBase **M**anagement **S**ystem):

  It is a database management system that organizes data into structured tables: each table is composed of rows and columns, where each row represents a data instance and each column represents an attribute or characteristic of the data itself.
  Relational databases are based on the theory of relations and use the relational model to manage data.
  The organization of data into relational tables allows for establishing logical relationships between them. These relationships are defined using primary keys and foreign keys, which connect the data across different tables.
  The connections between tables can be established through JOIN operations, which allow combining data from multiple tables based on specific criteria, facilitating the extraction of related information.

  Relational databases offer numerous advantages:

  1. They provide a rigid and consistent structure for organizing data. This means that data is defined and bound to a specific schema, ensuring consistency and integrity of the data itself. This is particularly important in business

contexts where maintaining data integrity and consistency is crucial.

2. They offer a range of advanced features for data management. These include data querying through the SQL language, which allows retrieving specific information from tables, filtering data based on certain criteria, and applying aggregation operations to obtain aggregated results.

3. They can ensure data integrity through referential integrity and data validation constraints. Referential integrity constraints ensure that the links between tables are correct, and that the data is consistent, while data validation constraints allow defining rules for accepting data based on certain criteria (e.g., a field must be an integer or a valid date).

- **Unstructured Database or NoSQL** (*UDBMS Ustructured DataBase Management System – Not only SQL*):

Unstructured databases play a fundamental role in managing unstructured or semi-structured data. This type of database is particularly suitable for handling a wide range of data, such as documents, images, audio, video, text messages, and other formats that do not conform to a rigid schema.

The main advantages offered by this type of database are:

1. They provide flexibility in data management:

Since they do not require a rigid schema, they allow for more dynamic storage and organization of data. This means that new types of data can be added, or the structure can be modified without reconfiguring the entire database. This flexibility is particularly useful in scenarios where data is constantly evolving or where different data sources with different formats need to be integrated.

2. They support greater scalability: They can handle very high data volumes, enabling the storage and management of large amounts of unstructured information. This scalability is crucial in the era of Big Data, where organizations need to deal with enormous amounts of data from various sources.

3. They allow for advanced searching and analysis of data: Through technologies like indexing and full-text search, specific information within unstructured data can be quickly retrieved. This enables in-depth analysis and obtaining meaningful insights from the data, contributing to informed decision-making.

4. They facilitate integration with other technologies such as artificial intelligence and machine learning: These technologies often require access to large amounts of unstructured data for model training. By using an unstructured database, the necessary data for these tasks can be easily stored, organized, and managed.

5. They enable harnessing the information contained in unstructured data: Analysis of unstructured data can reveal new business opportunities, identify emerging trends, enhance customer experience, and optimize business processes.

- **Graph Database** (*GDBMS Graph DataBase Management System*):
  Graph databases are a type of database that is based on the concept of visually representing objects and their relationships.
  The main advantages of graph databases include the ability to effectively model and analyze relationships between objects, high performance in complex queries, flexibility in data modeling, scalability to handle large volumes of interconnected data, and a wide range of practical applications.
  Leveraging graph databases can lead to a better understanding of complex data, enabling the discovery of meaningful insights and informed decision-making based on object relationships.
  This type of database is particularly suitable for managing complex and interconnected data, such as social networks, concept maps, transportation networks, and many other scenarios where object relationships are fundamental.

Let's analyze some of the mentioned advantages of this type of database:

1. The ability to effectively model and analyze relationships between objects: By using nodes to represent objects and edges to represent relationships, graph databases allow capturing

and representing complex connections between data in a clear and intuitive manner. This facilitates pattern detection, discovery of hidden relationships, and analysis of interactions between objects.

2. They offer high performance in executing complex queries on relationships: Thanks to the graph structure and optimized algorithms for node traversal and search operations, it is possible to efficiently execute queries that involve navigating between objects and calculating their connections. This results in reduced response times and high performance when working with complex and interconnected data.

3. Flexibility in data modeling: Unlike relational databases that require a rigid and predefined schema, graph databases allow adding or modifying relationships between objects without restructuring the entire database schema. This flexibility is particularly useful in scenarios where data undergoes frequent changes or when exploring different perspectives on the data is necessary.

4. They are highly scalable: They can easily handle large volumes of interconnected data and support the expansion of data quantity and relationships over time. This makes them suitable for applications where data growth is expected or where managing a vast amount of connections between objects is necessary.

Use cases

Each type of database offers specific advantages and is used in different use cases. The specific advantages and use cases for each type of database are:

- Relational databases provide a well-defined structure and the ability to perform JOIN operations to extract complex information from the data. They are suitable for business applications that require strict data organization and management of complex transactions.

- Unstructured databases are flexible and suitable for handling unstructured or semi-structured data, such as documents or media. They are widely used in content management applications, media streaming, and storage of unstructured data.

- Graph databases are particularly suitable for managing interconnected data, such as social networks or concept maps. They allow analyzing complex relationships between objects and performing efficient queries to identify connections and patterns.

Lineage & ETL

Common technical terms:

1. **Data Lineage:**
   The traceability of the origins and transformations of data over time.

2. **ETL:**
   Extract, Transform, Load, a process for extracting, transforming, and loading data from various sources into a target system.

3. **Data Source:**
   A data provider from which data is extracted.

4. **Data Transformation:**
   The process of modifying data to make it consistent and suitable for the intended use.

In the world of data management, data lineage and the ETL (Extract, Transform, Load) process play a crucial role in managing and using data. In this chapter, we will delve into the importance of data lineage and the ETL process in ensuring reliable and consistent data.

Data Lineage

Data lineage provides a comprehensive and transparent framework of the origin and transformations of data along its path. It is essential for ensuring data quality, integrity, and compliance, as well as supporting accurate decision-making processes and reliable analysis.

Here are some key points to further explore the concept:

1. *Audit and regulatory compliance*:
   Data lineage is crucial for demonstrating compliance with regulations and company policies. Tracking the origin and transformations of data allows for detailed documentation of data sources, applied governance rules, and modifications made. This is particularly relevant in regulatory contexts, such as the European Union's General Data Protection Regulation (GDPR), which requires the ability to demonstrate the lawful use of personal data.

2. *Data analysis and data science*:
   It is vital for data scientists and analysts who want to understand the data transformation process and reproduce results. It enables the verification of analysis validity, identification of potential errors or discrepancies in data transformations, and the ability to replicate the analysis using updated or modified data.

3. **Risk management and issue resolution:**
   Data lineage is valuable in risk management and
   resolving data-related issues. In case of errors or
   problems in results, the traceability of lineage helps
   trace back to data sources, applied transformations,
   and critical steps that may have caused the error.
   This simplifies error detection and correction,
   improving data quality and confidence in analyses.

4. **Data governance e data quality:**
   Data lineage is a key element of data governance. It
   provides a detailed view of data dependencies and
   relationships, enabling organizations to make
   informed decisions about data management,
   storage, and usage. Additionally, it helps assess data
   quality by identifying any issues or errors in
   transformations that could impact data integrity.

ETL

The **E**xtract, **T**ransform, **L**oad (*ETL*) process is a
fundamental methodology for acquiring, transforming, and
loading data into a usable format. It consists of three key
phases that allow for managing and preparing data for
analysis and operational use:

1. **Extraction:**
   In the extraction phase, data is retrieved from the
   source systems, which can be databases, files, web
   services, or other external systems. The main goal is
   to select and gather the relevant data needed for a
   specific analysis or to fulfill application requirements.
   During this phase, it's important to define extraction
   criteria, such as filters or queries, to obtain only the

desired data and reduce the amount of transferred data.

2. **Transformation**:
   In the transformation phase, the extracted data undergoes various transformations to make it consistent, clean, and ready for use. These transformations can include operations such as data normalization, cleaning inconsistent or missing values, deduplication, aggregation, creating new derived variables, or applying specific business rules. The objective is to create a consistent and high-quality data structure that can support the desired analyses and applications.

3. **Loading:**
   In the loading phase, the transformed data is loaded into a target system, such as a data warehouse, data mart, or analytics application. During loading, the data can be organized and structured appropriately, following a defined schema, to make it easily accessible and usable by end-users. It's important to ensure that the target system can handle the volume and speed of data loading, ensuring data integrity and consistency within the system.

Importance of ETL and Lineage

The combination of data lineage and the ETL process plays a critical role in ensuring data consistency, reliability, and quality. The traceability provided by data lineage allows understanding the origin and history of the data, while the ETL process ensures that the data is clean, structured, and ready for use by end-users. This synergy is crucial for making informed decisions, conducting accurate analyses, and effectively managing the data lifecycle.

1. ***Data Traceability and Consistency***:
   Data lineage enables tracing the origin and history of the data, providing a comprehensive view of its transformations throughout the ETL process. This helps identify and rectify any errors or discrepancies that may have been introduced during the data extraction, transformation, or loading phases. Data lineage traceability is particularly useful for troubleshooting activities as it allows quickly pinpointing the causes of errors and restoring data consistency.

2. ***Data Cleansing and Standardization***:
   The ETL process includes the data transformation phase, where cleansing and standardization rules are applied to ensure data uniformity and consistent structure. Data lineage provides an overview of the transformations performed, such as removing duplicate values, correcting formatting errors, or adding new derived columns. This helps improve data quality and ensures they are ready for use in analyses and decision-making processes.

3. ***Data Preparation for End-Users***:
   The combination of data lineage and the ETL process is essential for making data ready for use by end-users. Through the ETL process, data is transformed and structured appropriately to meet specific user needs. Data lineage provides a complete picture of the applied transformations, allowing end-users to understand the context and reliability of the data they are using. This fosters trust in data usage and

facilitates informed decision-making.

4. ***Data Monitoring and Management*:**
The combination of data lineage and the ETL process also enables data monitoring and management over time. Data lineage traceability helps maintain a record of data changes and transformations, enabling effective data lifecycle management. Additionally, data lineage can be used for data quality audit and control, contributing to ensuring compliance with business rules and regulations.

Data Quality

Common technical terms:

1. ***Data profiling:***
   The statistical and structural analysis of data to identify anomalies, missing values, or inconsistencies, in order to assess data quality.

2. ***Data sampling:***
   The selection of a representative subset of data to evaluate its quality, particularly useful when analyzing the entire dataset is resource-intensive or impractical.

3. ***Compliance assessment:***
   The analysis of data against predefined rules and standards to verify data compliance with those rules and identify quality issues.

4. **Data Standardization:**
   The application of standardization rules to ensure data consistency, such as standardizing date formats or currencies, to facilitate data integration and analysis from different sources.

Data quality is a fundamental element for the success of organizations in the information age. Measuring and improving data quality can help make more informed decisions, improve operational efficiency, and build a solid reputation. Investing in data quality management is an important step in ensuring the value and reliability of the information that drives the company.

Measuring data quality

Measuring data quality is a crucial step in identifying issues and areas for improvement.
There are several aspects of data quality and methodologies to manage them that can be considered:

- **Data profiling:**
  Involves statistical and structural analysis of the data to identify anomalies, missing values, or inconsistencies.
  EG: analyzing missing values in a field can reveal data completeness, while analyzing out-of-range values can highlight data accuracy.

- **Data sampling:**
  Involves selecting a representative subset of data to evaluate its quality. This can be useful when analyzing the entire dataset is resource-intensive or

impractical.

EG: sampling records from a sales dataset and comparing them with external sources can assess data accuracy.

- **Compliance assessment:**
  Involves analyzing data against predefined rules and standards.
  EG: defining validation rules for dataset fields and verifying data compliance with those rules. Inconsistency between the data and established rules may indicate quality issues.

- **Data standardization:**
  Applying standardization rules helps ensure consistency.
  EG: standardizing date or currency formats can facilitate data integration and analysis from different sources.

- **Data cleansing:**
  Data cleansing involves identifying and correcting errors, duplicate values, or inconsistencies. This may require the use of matching algorithms or deduplication techniques to identify duplicate records and resolve any discrepancies.

- **Implementation of data quality controls:**
  Implementing data quality controls during data entry or update processes can help prevent errors and improve overall quality.
  EG: defining validation checks for mandatory fields or specific data formats.

- **User training and awareness:**
  A key element in ensuring data quality is training staff and promoting a data quality-oriented company

culture. Raising awareness among users about the importance of data quality and providing training on proper data management procedures can help reduce errors and improve overall data quality.

Improving data quality

Improving data quality is an ongoing process that requires continuous commitment from the organization. Investing in the necessary resources, processes, and tools to enhance data quality can lead to numerous benefits, including more informed decisions, increased operational efficiency, and a better corporate reputation.

Here are some suggestions for improving data quality:

- **Standardize data entry processes**:
  Establishing clear procedures for data collection, entry, and updates can help reduce errors and improve data consistency.
  EG: *Define a common format for dates or product codes.*

- **Automate data quality checks:**
  Using specialized tools and software can streamline and automate data quality control processes. These tools can perform automated checks on entered data, detect anomalies, and send notifications in case of quality issues.

- **Continuously monitor data quality:**
  Data quality is not a one-time achievement but requires continuous monitoring over time. It is important to define data quality metrics and

constantly monitor the data to identify any issues or discrepancies. This can be done through the implementation of reports and dashboards that provide a real-time overview of data quality.
EG: Verify that a phone number is in the correct format or that an email address contains "@" and a valid domain. Additionally, regularly perform data cleansing processes to eliminate duplicates, incorrect or inconsistent values.

- **Implement a data governance system:**
  Data governance involves implementing policies, procedures, and controls to ensure data quality. This may include appointing data quality officers, defining quality standards and metrics, and establishing monitoring and reporting processes.

- **Foster collaboration and communication among teams:**
  Promoting a culture of collaboration and communication among teams handling data can facilitate information exchange and early identification of errors or discrepancies. Sharing best practices and aligning across different teams can contribute to overall data quality improvement.

- **Feedback and iterations:**
  Gathering feedback from users and stakeholders can be a valuable tool for improving data quality. Active involvement of users in reporting errors or issues can help identify areas for improvement and implement corrective actions.

Examples of the impact of data quality

It is evident that data quality can have a significant impact on the effectiveness and overall success of a company.

Investing in data quality management and improvement can help avoid costly errors, improve productivity, meet regulatory requirements, and maintain a good corporate reputation.
To better understand this, let's consider some examples of how low-quality data can influence different business situations:

- *Decisions based on inaccurate data:*
  If the data used to make business decisions is incorrect or incomplete, the decisions themselves may be flawed or ineffective, leading to negative outcomes for the company.

- *Customer relationship management issues:*
  Low-quality data in the customer database can result in communication problems, sending incorrect or repetitive messages, or even losing customers due to inaccurate or outdated information.

- *Impact on company reputation:*
  Inaccurate or outdated data can have a negative impact on the company's reputation in the eyes of customers, business partners, or regulatory authorities.

- *Missed business opportunities:*
  Incomplete or incorrect data can lead to missed business opportunities.

EG: if the contact data of potential customers is not correct, it may be impossible to reach them for business proposals or to offer products or services.

- **Risk of non-compliance:**
  Low-quality data can put the company at risk of non-compliance with regulations and standards.
  EG: n the case of the General Data Protection Regulation (GDPR), the lack of accurate and up-to-date data can result in privacy rule violations and subsequent penalties.

- **Additional costs for data correction:**
  Correcting low-quality data can require significant time and resources.
  EG: if a customer database needs to be cleaned of duplicate or inconsistent data, resources will need to be allocated to identify and rectify them.

Bigdata

Common technical terms:

1. **Data Warehouse:**
   A centralized system for storing data for business analysis.

2. **Data Lake:**
   A repository of raw, structured, and unstructured data without a rigid schema.

3. **Data Mesh:**
   A decentralized approach to data management that promotes data ownership and responsibility to the teams that generate them.

In the increasingly digitized world we live in, the amount of data generated and collected has grown exponentially. This phenomenon has led to the emergence of a fundamental concept: Big Data.

The emergence of Big Data

The emergence of Big Data has been driven by several factors that have led to an explosion in the quantity and variety of available data.

Increased connectivity and widespread access to digital devices such as smartphones, tablets, and IoT sensors have made it possible to continuously generate data from various sources. Simultaneously, technological advancements have provided the necessary tools to capture, store, and process large volumes of data.

Storage capacities and computing power of computer systems have significantly increased, enabling the management and analysis of data at an unprecedented scale.

Additionally, the development of advanced algorithms and data analysis techniques has made it possible to extract meaningful information and insights from Big Data.

The wide variety of data available in Big Data is particularly significant. In addition to traditional structured data such as tables and databases, there is also unstructured data such as text, images, audio, and video. This variety of formats and content offers opportunities for integrated and multidimensional analysis, enabling the discovery of correlations, hidden patterns, and insights that may otherwise be overlooked.

Big Data offers numerous benefits and opportunities in various sectors:

- In the healthcare sector, data analysis can contribute to the discovery of new treatments, prediction of epidemics, and monitoring the effectiveness of healthcare.

- In the financial sector, Big Data analysis can help detect fraud, predict market trends, and support investment decisions.

- In the financial sector, Big Data analysis can help detect fraud, predict market trends, and support investment decisions.

The use of Big Data also presents significant challenges. Managing, processing, and analyzing large quantities of data require advanced infrastructure and technologies, as well as specific expertise in data management and analysis. Additionally, issues related to data privacy and security must be addressed, ensuring that appropriate measures are taken to protect sensitive information.

The 5 "V"

Big Data is characterized by five main dimensions known as the "5 V's": *V*olume, *V*elocity, *V*ariety, *V*eracity, and *V*alue:

- *Volume* refers to the vast amount of data generated, often exceeding the capacity of traditional data management systems.

- *Velocity* concerns the speed at which data is generated and needs to be processed in real-time or near real-time.

- *Variety* refers to the diversity of data types and sources, which can include text, images, videos, geospatial data, and more.

- **Veracity** represents the challenge of ensuring the reliability and accuracy of data, considering the possibility of errors, incompleteness, and falsification.

- **Value** is linked to the idea that the collected and analyzed data must have some form of utility or relevance to justify the investment of time, resources, and efforts in their management and analysis.

From Data Warehouse to Data Lake to Data Mesh

In the past, data was often stored in centralized, structured data warehouses organized according to a defined schema.

The transition from Data Warehouse to Data Lake and subsequently to Data Mesh represents a logical progression in data management.

The concept of a Data Lake revolutionized data management by allowing the storage of large quantities of raw, structured, and unstructured data without the need for a predefined structure.
The Data Lake facilitated the aggregation of data from various sources into a single platform, providing a centralized repository accessible to different business functions.
This approach offered greater flexibility in data access and analysis, enabling organizations to explore and discover

new insights without the restrictions of a rigid schema. However, the Data Lake can present challenges such as data fragmentation and complexity in managing unstructured data.

This is where the concept of Data Mesh comes into play, promoting the distribution of data among teams and business units, sharing the responsibility for data management in a more autonomous manner.
In the context of Data Mesh, each team becomes the owner of their own data and adopts data management practices based on common principles, standards, and shared tools.
This decentralized approach encourages collaboration among teams, promotes innovation, and reduces dependence on a single central control point.

With Data Mesh, guidelines and standards are provided to ensure interoperability of distributed data. This facilitates integration and data sharing among teams, enabling a holistic view of enterprise data. Additionally, the adoption of common data management tools promotes efficiency and security in accessing distributed data.

The key benefits of the Data Mesh concept include increased business agility, as teams can make autonomous decisions regarding the management of their own data without relying on centralized processes.
This accelerates response times and enables organizations to quickly adapt to changing needs and new challenges.

Data Mesh greatly facilitates sharing and collaboration among teams, fostering a work environment based on mutual trust and shared responsibility.
This approach stimulates innovation, allowing teams to independently explore data and discover new insights without restrictions.

From a technological standpoint, Data Mesh offers greater scalability, enabling companies to handle large volumes of data and efficiently distribute it among teams.
This is particularly important in the context of Big Data, where the amount of generated and collected data continues to grow exponentially.

Data Fabric

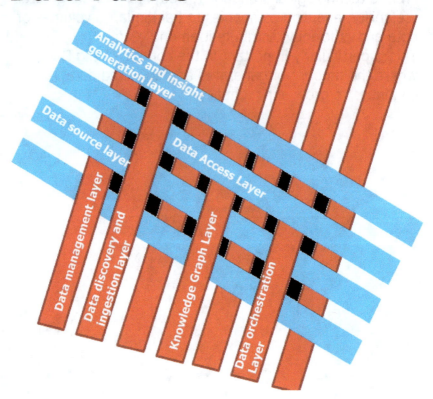

Common technical terms:

1. **Data Integration:**
   The process of combining and consolidating data from various sources.

2. **Distributed Data Architecture:**
   A system in which data is distributed across multiple nodes or clusters for scalable management.

3. **Data Governance:**
   The policies and processes to ensure data quality, security, and compliance.

The Data Fabric represents a modern and comprehensive methodology for data management, enabling organizations to effectively handle the vast amount of available data and fully leverage its potential. Using integrated components and a unified view of data, the Data Fabric provides a robust infrastructure to support data processing, analysis, and data-driven decision-making in an agile and efficient manner.

What is Data Fabric

The concept of Data Fabric emerged in the early 2000s as a response to the growing demand from businesses to manage data in a distributed and often complex environment. As the needs of corporate data evolved, companies had to contend with these new complexities, their heterogeneous nature, and the fact that they resided in multiple applications and environments scattered throughout the entire business ecosystem. The term "fabric" refers to the construction of a fabric composed of multiple threads, each representing a data source, and the fabric is then used as a foundation for data processing.

Areas of Data Fabric

According to Forrester research (*Unleash Your Growth Potential with Continuous Planning*, 2017), 90% of companies believe real-time decision-making is a crucial component for market success. With data fabric enabling self-service data management and automation of lengthy manual data management processes, both necessary for real-time or near-real-time decision-making, its adoption becomes a matter of "*when*" rather than "*why*."

Research conducted by leading industry agencies shows

that the economic impact of inaccurate data can cost companies up to 30% of their revenue: missed sales opportunities resulting from inaccurate customer records, incorrect credit score calculations due to erroneous data input into ML algorithms, overpayments to employees due to incomplete and disorganized payroll records. These are just some of the potential consequences of poor-quality information.

Data fabric tackles this challenge by incorporating AI and ML capabilities for continuous data quality refinement. Companies need to step back and examine data management holistically through a data fabric architecture. While data fabric is not a complete solution, it significantly reduces the work associated with meeting compliance requirements.

Key Components of Data Fabric

The Data Fabric comprises several components that work synergistically to create a cohesive data management environment.
The main components include:

- ***Data integration tools***:
  These tools enable the acquisition and integration of data from various sources, facilitating the connection and harmonization of heterogeneous data.

- ***Distributed data architectures***:
  Distributed data architectures allow data to be distributed across multiple nodes or clusters, ensuring scalability and operational resilience.

- **Data governance tools:**
  These tools ensure the quality, security, and compliance of data within the Data Fabric, providing control and governance mechanisms.

- **Analytics and Artificial Intelligence Tools:**
  These tools enable advanced data processing and analysis within the Data Fabric, paving the way for meaningful insights and the application of predictive models.

The synergistic interaction of these components forms a robust and adaptable Data Fabric that can be tailored to the specific needs of an organization.

Business Intelligence

Common technical terms:

1. **Business Intelligence (BI):**
   A set of processes, technologies, and tools for acquiring, analyzing, and presenting business data to support decision-making.

2. **Data Warehouse:**
   A centralized repository of data from various sources used for analysis and report generation.

3. **OLAP:**
   Online Analytical Processing, an approach to data analysis that allows interacting with data in a multidimensional manner.

4. **Dashboard:**
   A visual interface that presents key information and business metrics in a clear and concise manner.

Business Intelligence (BI) is a strategic discipline for businesses aiming to support data-driven decision-making.

Let's delve further into the concept of Business Intelligence and the three key aspects contributing to its effectiveness:

What is BI (Business Intelligence)

Business Intelligence is a set of processes, tools, and technologies that enable organizations to acquire, manage, analyze, and present business data in a meaningful way. It is based on the idea of transforming raw data into useful and relevant information to support planning, performance analysis, risk assessment, and strategic decision-making. BI involves collecting data from various sources, transforming them into understandable formats, and distributing them through reports, dashboards, and visualization tools. By using data warehouses, OLAP, data visualization, and KPIs, BI provides a clear overview of business performance, facilitating the identification of improvement opportunities and proactive adaptation to market challenges.

Data warehouse and OLAP

In the context of Business Intelligence, data warehouses and OLAP (*OnLine Analytical Processing*) play a fundamental role in data analysis. A data warehouse is a centralized repository that gathers data from different sources, integrates them, and organizes them to facilitate analysis and reporting. It represents a valuable resource for accessing and analyzing historical business data. On the other hand, OLAP is a technology that enables analyzing data in a multidimensional manner. Through OLAP, interactive and complex queries can be performed to explore data from various perspectives, such as by period, product, region, or other attributes. This allows users to gain an in-depth view of the data and identify significant patterns or trends

Data Visualization and KPIs

Data visualization and the use of KPI (*Key Performance Indicators*) are key elements for understanding business performance in Business Intelligence. Data visualization refers to the visual representation of data through charts, diagrams, tables, or other visual forms. This allows presenting data in an intuitive and understandable way, facilitating the communication of information and enabling users to interpret data more effectively.

KPIs are key measures that reflect business performance against specific objectives or success indicators. They can be represented through pie charts, bar graphs, or colored indicators to highlight target achievement. KPIs enable monitoring business performance in a quick and visual manner, providing an immediate picture of progress and compliance with objectives.

Data Science

Common technical terms:

1. ***Data Science:***
   A field that combines scientific methods, statistics, and computer science to extract knowledge and insights from data.

2. ***Data Mining:***
   The extraction of patterns and useful information through statistical analysis techniques and complex algorithms.

3. ***Machine Learning:***
   A field of artificial intelligence that deals with the development of algorithms that allow computers to learn and improve from experiences.

4. ***Predictive Model:***
   A statistical model or Machine Learning algorithm that uses historical data to make predictions about the future.

Data Science (DS) plays a fundamental role in uncovering insights from data: it is a discipline that combines knowledge of statistics, mathematics, computer science, and domain expertise to extract meaningful information. Through the process of data acquisition, cleaning, analysis, and interpretation, it enables extracting significant knowledge from data that can support informed decision-making.

The use of Machine Learning algorithms and predictive models enhances the capabilities of Data Science, allowing for forecasting and identifying complex patterns in data.

The primary role of Data Science is to transform raw data into usable knowledge.

By using analytical techniques and models, Data Science enables a better understanding of data, predicts future behavior, identifies correlations, and uncovers patterns that may not be evident through simple data observation.

The DS Process

The Data Science process follows a series of stages that include data acquisition, cleaning, analysis, and interpretation.
Data acquisition involves collecting raw data from various sources such as databases, files, or sensors. These data can be structured (e.g., database tables) or unstructured (e.g., free text).
Data cleaning is a critical phase where the data undergoes filtering and correction processes to ensure accuracy, completeness, and consistency. This may involve handling missing values, resolving formatting errors, or managing outliers.

Data analysis involves applying algorithms and statistical methods to identify significant patterns, relationships, or trends in the data. This may include using data visualization techniques to make the collected information more understandable.
Data interpretation involves analyzing the results obtained from the analysis and translating them into comprehensible knowledge and insights.

This step helps in making informed decisions based on the results obtained from Data Science.

Machine Learning and Predictive Models

In the field of Data Science, Machine Learning algorithms and predictive models play a crucial role in processing data and obtaining useful information for informed decision-making.

Machine Learning algorithms are a set of techniques and procedures that enable computers to learn automatically from data without being explicitly programmed for specific tasks. These algorithms can recognize patterns, identify relationships, and make predictions based on the training data.

Training a Machine Learning algorithm involves providing the computer with a training dataset, which consists of input examples and their corresponding labels or desired outcomes.
The algorithm analyzes this data and tries to identify hidden patterns or relationships between the input and output. Once trained, the algorithm can be used to make

predictions on new data based on the patterns learned during the training phase.

Predictive models, on the other hand, are built based on existing data to make predictions or estimate future values. These models are often based on Machine Learning algorithms but can also use statistical or mathematical approaches to identify relationships and trends in the data. Predictive models can be used in a wide range of applications such as sales forecasting, risk analysis, resource optimization, fraud detection, and more.

To build a predictive model, it is necessary to select relevant input variables, train the model using available training data, and then evaluate the model's performance using validation or test data.
Once the model is adequately trained and validated, it can be used to make predictions on new data, allowing users to obtain estimates and forecasts based on historical information and patterns identified in the training dataset.

Data Visualization

Common technical terms:

1. **Interactive visualizations**:
   Graphical representations of data that allow users to interact directly with the visual element to explore and analyze data in different ways.

2. **Self-service Analytics:**
   The ability for users to explore and analyze data independently without requiring advanced technical skills.

3. **Dynamic charts:**
   Visual representations of data that can be updated in real time or in response to user interactions, allowing

for flexible and customizable data visualization.

Data visualization, or data viz, is the process of visually representing data and information through charts, tables, diagrams, and other visual elements.

The main goal of data visualization is to communicate effectively the patterns, relationships, and trends present in data, allowing users to understand and interpret information in a more intuitive and immediate way.

What are its uses

Data visualization is a key role in the exploration and understanding of data, providing a visual representation that simplifies the complexity of information.

Here are some of the main reasons why data visualization is important:

- ***Information synthesis***:
  It helps to synthesize large amounts of complex information concisely.
  Through charts and diagrams, data can be presented in a structured way, making it easier to understand and interpret.

- ***Identification of patterns and trends:***
  It allows to identify patterns, correlations and hidden trends in the data. Interactive charts and dynamic visualizations allow users to explore data from different perspectives and discover relationships that might otherwise go unnoticed.

- ***Effective communication***:
  It is a powerful communication tool. Visual

representations can make data more accessible and engaging for a non-technical audience, making it easier to share information and communicate the results of analysis.

Data visualization is used in different industries and contexts, including:

- **_Businesses and organizations_**:
  Businesses use data visualization to monitor business performance, analyze market data, identify business opportunities, and communicate results to stakeholders.

- **_Healthcare_**:
  It is used to analyze clinical data, track the spread of diseases, monitor public health indicators, and support clinical decision-making.

- **_Financial sector_**:
  Financial institutions use data visualization to analyze market data, monitor financial trends, assess risks, and make informed investment decisions.

- **_Media sector_**:
  Journalists and editors use data visualization to illustrate complex stories and present data in a engaging way to readers.

Some Tools

The data visualization market is constantly evolving.

Here are 5 of the most popular and widely used tools at the moment:

- ***Tableau***:
  One of the leading data visualization tools on the market. It offers advanced features to create interactive visualizations, dashboards, and reports. It supports a wide range of data sources and offers sharing and collaboration options.

- ***Power BI***:
  Developed by Microsoft, it is another popular data visualization tool. It allows you to create interactive dashboards, reports, and custom visualizations. It also supports integration with other Microsoft applications such as Excel and Azure.

- ***QlikView***:
  A data visualization solution that allows you to create interactive visualizations and dynamic dashboards. It offers self-service analytics features and allows you to explore data intuitively.

- ***D3.js***:
  A JavaScript library for creating custom and interactive visualizations. It is widely used by developers to create custom and highly flexible visualizations.

- ***Google Data Studio***:
  A web-based data visualization tool that allows you to create interactive reports and dashboards using data from various sources. It offers sharing and collaboration features with other users.

Open Source Vs Enterprise

Both Open Source and Enterprise tools have their pros and cons, and the choice will depend on the needs, resources, and preferences of the organization intending to use them.

Open Source

Pros:

- *Affordability:*
  Most open-source tools are free or low-cost, making them accessible even to organizations with limited resources.

- *Flexibility:*
  They often offer greater flexibility to adapt to the specific needs of an organization.

- *Community and active support:*
  They benefit from active developer communities that contribute to the continuous improvement of the software and provide technical support.

Cons:

- *Learning curve:*
  some tools may require a steeper learning curve, especially for non-expert users.

- *Limited technical support:*
  Compared to enterprise software vendors, open-source tools tend to offer limited technical support or rely mainly on the user community for help.

Enterprise

Pros:

- *Dedicated technical support:*
  Enterprise software vendors usually offer dedicated technical support to assist users in the implementation and use of the tools.

- *Scalability:*
  Enterprise tools are designed to handle large amounts of data and can scale to meet the growing needs of the organization.

- *Security:*
  Enterprise software often provides advanced features to ensure data security and regulatory compliance.

Cons:

- *Costs:*
  Enterprise tools can be significantly expensive in terms of licenses, implementation, and maintenance.

- *Vendor dependency:*
  Using enterprise tools can lead to a greater dependency on the software vendor and limit the flexibility in adapting the software to the specific needs of the organization.

GDPR

Common technical terms:

1. **GDPR** (**G**eneral **D**ata **P**rotection **R**egulation)**:**
    a regulation of the European Union that regulates the protection of personal data and privacy of individuals in the EU.

2. **Consent:**
    The explicit and informed authorization provided by data subjects for the processing of their personal data.

4. **Transparency:**
    The obligation of organizations to provide clear and

*comprehensible information on the processing of
personal data.*

5. **Rights of data subjects:**
   *The rights granted to individuals by the GDPR, such
   as the right to access, the right to rectify, and the
   right to be forgotten.*

The *General Data Protection Regulation* (GDPR) is a
regulation in force in the European Union (EU) that aims to
protect the privacy and personal data of individuals within
the EU. It went into effect on May 25, 2018.
The GDPR was introduced to address the challenges and
concerns related to privacy and data security in the digital
age.

The need for a regulation like the GDPR was highlighted by
the increasing use and diffusion of personal data in the
context of commercial and online activities.

Before the introduction of the GDPR, privacy laws were
regulated at the national level within the individual
countries of the European Union, leading to a lack of
harmonization and an inconsistent protection of personal
data.

The GDPR was proposed by the European Commission in
January 2012 and subsequently adopted by the European
Parliament in 2016. Its introduction required a two-year
transition period to allow companies to adapt to the new
provisions.

The GDPR introduced several requirements and obligations
for companies that process personal data, including
fundamental principles such as informed consent, data
collection transparency, data minimization, data security,

and individuals' right to control their personal data.

With the GDPR, significant sanctions were introduced for violations of data protection provisions, with fines that can reach very high amounts. This has made the GDPR a powerful deterrent for organizations that do not comply with privacy standards.

The GDPR has had a significant impact globally, affecting not only European companies but also those that operate internationally and process personal data of European citizens: it has placed emphasis on the protection of personal data as a fundamental right and has pushed many organizations to review and improve their data privacy policies and practices.

Fundamental principles of the GDPR

The GDPR is based on some fundamental principles that guide the processing of personal data.
These principles include:

1. *Consent*:
   Companies must obtain the explicit and informed consent of individuals before collecting or using their personal data. Consent must be voluntary and specific for each purpose of data use.

2. *Transparency*:
   Companies must provide clear and comprehensible information on how personal data is processed, including purposes, duration, and recipients of the information.

3. *Individuals' rights*:
   The GDPR confers on citizens of the European Union several rights in relation to their personal data. These rights include the right to access their data, the right to rectify, the right to be forgotten (i.e., the right to request the deletion of their data), and the right to data portability.

Requirements and responsibilities of organizations

Organizations are required to meet a number of requirements to comply with the GDPR.

These requirements include:

1. *Designation of a data protection officer (DPO)*:
   Companies must designate a data protection officer (DPO) who is responsible for the management and monitoring of personal data processing.

2. *Data protection impact assessment (DPIA)*:
   Companies must conduct a data protection impact assessment to identify and mitigate the risks associated with personal data processing.

3. *Data Security*:
   Companies must implement adequate security measures to protect personal data from unauthorized access, loss, or breaches.

4. *Data breach notification*:
   In the event of a personal data breach, companies

must notify the competent supervisory authority within 72 hours of the discovery of the breach, unless the breach does not pose a risk to the rights and freedoms of individuals.

Establishing protocols to promptly notify the authorities and individuals involved in the event of a data breach helps to mitigate potential damage and demonstrates a commitment to transparency.

Right to be forgotten

Common technical terms:

1. ***Right to be Forgotten:***
   The right of individuals to request the deletion or removal of their personal data from an organization.

2. ***Data storage:***
   The process of storing data securely for a defined period.

3. ***Data retention:***
   The process of maintaining data for a longer period, often for legal or regulatory purposes.

This concept has gained notoriety and attention in recent years, especially following a landmark decision made by the Court of Justice of the European Union (CJEU):

In 2014, the CJEU issued a judgment that established an individual's right to request the removal of links to personal information deemed outdated, irrelevant, or no longer relevant.

This judgment was based on the case "*Google Spain v. AEPD and Mario Costeja González*," in which a Spanish citizen, Mario Costeja González, asked Google to remove links to a newspaper article that mentioned his previous property repossession.

The CJEU's judgment recognized that individuals have the right to control information concerning their private life and that the right to privacy may outweigh the public interest in accessing such information.
It ruled that search engines like Google can be considered responsible for disseminating such information and may be obliged to remove links if individuals' requests meet certain requirements.

The judgment led to the introduction of guidelines by the European Union's data protection authority to regulate the implementation of the right to be forgotten.
The guidelines established criteria for evaluating requests to remove links, considering factors such as the relevance and public interest of the information, the individual's legitimate interest, and the role played by the person in the event in question.

Subsequently, the CJEU's judgment influenced data protection legislation in Europe, including the introduction of the General Data Protection Regulation (GDPR) in 2018. The GDPR incorporated the right to be forgotten as one of the rights of individuals concerning their personal data.

What is the Right to Be Forgotten

The "Right to Be Forgotten" is a legal concept that refers to an individual's right to request the removal of specific personal information from online publication or access. This right is based on the idea that people should have control over their personal data and the right to decide when and how such data should be retained and used. The right to be forgotten is particularly important in personal data management because it gives individuals greater control over their privacy: it allows them to request the erasure of data that is no longer relevant, obsolete, or that they simply want to remove. This can be helpful in situations where personal data has been collected or used without consent or inappropriately.

Exercising the Right and Responsibilities of Companies

To exercise the right to be forgotten, an individual typically needs to submit a formal request to the organization responsible for their personal data. The company is then required to assess the request and, if appropriate, proceed with the deletion or removal of the requested data.

Companies have a responsibility to respect the right to be forgotten and handle requests promptly and effectively. They must establish internal processes and procedures to handle such requests and ensure that personal data is deleted in compliance with applicable regulatory provisions.

Impacts on Data Storage and Retention

The right to be forgotten can have a significant impact on data storage and retention operations: companies must be able to identify and isolate an individual's personal data to fulfill deletion requests.

However, it is essential to note that the right to be forgotten is not absolute and must be balanced with other legitimate purposes of data retention, such as complying with legal obligations or preserving data for historical or statistical purposes.
Therefore, companies must carefully evaluate deletion requests and determine if there are legal grounds for retaining data in certain contexts.

Public Data, Private Data and Sensitive Data

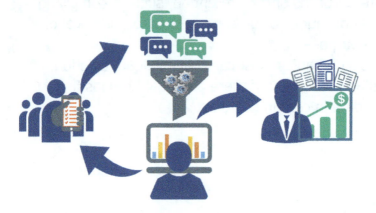

Common technical terms:

1. **Public Data:** Data accessible to the public without restrictions or limitations.

2. **Private Data:**
   Data that concerns identifiable personal information and is subject to privacy regulations.

3. **Sensitive Data:**
   Data that includes confidential or particularly sensitive information, such as financial or health-related information.

The distinction between public, private, and sensitive data is essential for understanding the implications related to data access, processing, and protection.
Companies have the responsibility to ensure that data is managed securely and in compliance with privacy regulations.
Awareness and proper management of sensitive data are

crucial to protecting the privacy of the individuals involved and maintaining trust in data management.

Data Types

Public data refers to information that is accessible to the public without specific restrictions. This may include government data, business information, demographic statistics, or any other freely available information. Public data is typically made available to promote transparency and information sharing.

Private data, on the other hand, refers to personal or confidential information owned by individuals or organizations. This data is generally subject to privacy rules and regulations and requires specific authorization for access and use. Examples of private data may include personal information like names, addresses, phone numbers, or financial data.

Sensitive data is a subcategory of private data that pertains to particularly delicate or risky information. This may include medical data, sensitive financial information, social security numbers, or biometric data. Sensitive data requires special protection due to its potential impact on the privacy or security of the individuals involved.

Access, Processing, and Protection:

Access, processing, and protection of data must be carefully considered based on their category. Public data is generally accessible to everyone without specific restrictions. However, it is important to ensure that it is reliable and sourced from official sources.

Private data requires limited access only to those with authorization. Organizations must adopt appropriate security measures to protect this data from unauthorized access or fraud.

Sensitive data demands the highest level of protection and confidentiality. Organizations must comply with privacy regulations and implement advanced security measures to safeguard this data from potential risks. This may include data encryption, role-based access and permissions, and rigorous management of sensitive data storage and transmission.

Company Responsibilities

Organizations that collect and use sensitive data have the responsibility to protect and use it ethically.

Prioritizing privacy, companies can build customer trust by upholding key values such as:

- *Transparency*:
  Clearly communicating how data is collected, used, and protected builds trust. Informing customers about privacy practices and obtaining their consent helps establish a transparent relationship.

- *Data Minimization*:
  Collecting only necessary data and minimizing the collection of personally identifiable information (PII) demonstrates respect for customer privacy.

- **_Privacy Policies_**:
  Providing easily accessible and comprehensive privacy policies that outline how customer data is managed and protected.

- **_Data Protection Measures_**:
  Implementing robust data security measures, such as:
  - _Data Anonymization_:
    Anonymization involves removing or encapsulating personally identifiable information (PII) from collected data. This process ensures that individuals cannot be directly identified from the data, thereby protecting their privacy.

  - _Encryption_:
    Encryption is the process of encoding data to make it unreadable to unauthorized parties. By encrypting data during storage and transmission, even if intercepted, the data remains secure and unusable to attackers.

  - _Access Controls_:
    Implementing access controls ensures that only authorized individuals can access sensitive data.
    This involves using usernames, passwords, and other authentication mechanisms to restrict data access based on user roles and permissions.

Additionally, organizations must adopt internal policies and procedures to ensure proper management of sensitive data. This may include appointing a data protection officer, implementing data retention policies, and providing staff training on best practices for data management.

Glossary

Below is an excerpt of the main terms used in data management (many of which you have encountered in this essay), grouped by macro areas of expertise, along with their respective meanings (it should be noted that, as you read earlier, these areas are closely interconnected).

Macro area: Database Administration & Management

- *Database*:
  A database is an organized collection of structured data that is stored and managed efficiently. It is designed to allow secure and reliable access,

management, and manipulation of data.

- **SQL**:
  SQL (*Structured Query Language*) is a programming language used to communicate with databases. It enables the creation, modification, and querying of data within a database, performing operations such as insertion, updating, deletion, and retrieval of data.

- **Query**:
  A query is a request for specific information or data from a database. Through SQL, you can formulate queries to obtain specific data that meets certain search criteria.

- **Schema**:
  In a database, a schema defines the structure and organization of the data. It includes information such as tables, fields, table relationships, and data constraints. The schema provides a description of how data is organized and linked within the database.

- **Table**:
  A table is a data structure in a database that represents a collection of records organized in rows and columns. Each column represents a specific data field, while each row contains the corresponding values for those fields for a particular record.

- **Primary Key**:
  A primary key is a field or a set of fields within a table that uniquely identifies each record. It is used to ensure the unique identification of records and establish relationships with other tables.

- ***Index***:
  An index is a data structure that speeds up the search and retrieval of data within a database. It is created on one or more fields of a table to allow quick access to data, reducing the need to scan the entire table.

- ***Backup***:
  A backup is a copy of data created to protect it from loss or damage. It involves making a copy of the data at a specific moment, so it can be restored in case of issues such as hardware failure, human error, or a cyber-attack.

- ***Restore***:
  Restoration refers to the process of recovering data or systems after a failure, error, or data loss. It involves using backup copies to restore data to its previous state before the problem occurred, in order to resume normal operations.

- ***Scalability***:
  Scalability refers to the ability of a system or infrastructure to effectively handle an increase in workload or data volume. A scalable system can manage increased demands without compromising performance, adapting to an organization's growing needs.

- ***Replication***:
  Replication is the process of creating and maintaining identical copies of data or resources in multiple locations. It is used for purposes such as data redundancy and availability, reducing data access times, and distributing the workload among

different servers or network nodes.

- **Data Integrity:**
  Data integrity refers to the correctness, coherence, and completeness of data. It ensures that data is accurate, reliable, and compliant with business rules or expected standards. Data integrity is maintained through validation rules, quality controls, and mechanisms to protect data from unauthorized changes or access.

Macro area: Business Intelligence

- **Data Warehouse:**
  A data warehouse is a centralized infrastructure for managing and analyzing data from various sources. It is designed to support the storage of large volumes of historical data, providing an optimized environment for processing and analyzing business data.

- **OLAP** (*Online Analytical Processing*):
  OLAP is a technology that allows interactive analysis of data from different perspectives.
  Through OLAP, users can explore and analyze multidimensional data flexibly, enabling them to formulate complex queries and obtain rapid answers.

- **ETL** (*Extract, Transform, Load*):
  ETL represents the process of extracting, transforming, and loading data from different sources into a data warehouse or another target system. Extraction involves retrieving data from sources, transformation entails processing and

cleaning the data, while loading involves loading transformed data into the target system.

- **Data Mart:**
  A data mart is a subset of a data warehouse that focuses on a specific area or a specific set of data for a particular department or user. A data mart is designed to provide quick and targeted access to relevant data for a specific purpose or analysis.

- **Data Mining:**
  Data mining is the process of discovering patterns, relationships, and useful information from data. Through advanced analysis techniques, data mining extracts hidden knowledge or meaningful insights from data, which can be used for informed decision-making or predictions.

- **KPI (Key Performance Indicator):**
  A KPI is a key performance indicator that measures the performance of an organization, process, or project. KPIs are measurable and quantifiable and are used to evaluate the effectiveness, efficiency, and success of a specific activity.

- **Dashboard:**
  A dashboard is a graphical interface that synthetically and intuitively displays key information and relevant data for a specific context or objective. Through graphs, tables, and visual indicators, a dashboard provides an immediate overview of important performance, metrics, and trends.

- **Data Visualization:**
  Data visualization is the graphical representation of data to facilitate understanding and communication

of information. Using graphs, charts, maps, and other visual representations, data visualization allows for more effective data exploration and communication, highlighting patterns, correlations, or key points.

Macro area: Data Science

- **_Machine Learning_**:
  Machine Learning is an area of artificial intelligence that deals with developing algorithms and models that enable computers to learn from data and improve performance over time without being explicitly programmed. Machine Learning is used for data analysis, classification, prediction, and many other applications.

- **_Algorithm_**:
  An algorithm is a series of instructions or rules followed to solve a problem or perform a specific task. In data management, algorithms are used to process data, identify patterns or relationships, conduct analysis, and make data-driven decisions.

- **_Predictive Model_**:
  A predictive model is a mathematical abstraction or representation of data used to make predictions or estimates about future events or outcomes based on historical data or identified patterns. Predictive models are constructed using Machine Learning techniques and applied to make forecasts in various sectors, such as marketing, finance, healthcare, etc.

- ***Big Data***:
  The term "Big Data" refers to large and complex data sets that require special tools and techniques for processing, analysis, and extracting value. Big Data is characterized by the five Vs: Volume (large data quantities), Velocity (data generation and flow speed), Variety (data types and sources diversity),Veracity (ensuring data quality) and Value (Utility and/or Data relevance).

- ***Data Governance***:
  Data Governance is a set of policies, processes, and procedures that define the management, quality, access, security, and use of data within an organization. Data Governance aims to ensure that data is managed effectively, securely, and compliant with regulations.

- ***Data Quality***:
  Data Quality refers to the extent to which data is accurate, reliable, and suitable for its intended use. Data Quality is influenced by factors such as data integrity, completeness, consistency, and accuracy. Good Data Quality is essential for making informed and reliable data-driven decisions.

- ***Hadoop***:
  Hadoop is an open-source framework used for distributed processing of large amounts of data. It provides a scalable platform for storing and processing Big Data on clusters of computers. Hadoop includes the Hadoop Distributed File System (HDFS: ***Hadoop Distributed File System***) and the MapReduce distributed processing framework.

- **NoSQL** (*Not only SQL*):
  NoSQL is a term that refers to a broad class of databases using data models different from the traditional relational model. NoSQL databases are designed to handle large volumes of unstructured or semi-structured data and offer greater scalability and flexibility than relational databases.

- **Cloud Computing**:
  Cloud Computing refers to the delivery of computing services over the Internet, enabling access to computing resources such as servers, storage, databases, and software on demand. Cloud Computing offers scalability, flexibility, and data accessibility from anywhere and any device without the need for physical infrastructure on-premises.

- **XML** (*eXtensible Markup Language*):
  It is a format that uses tags to define the structure of data. Each element is enclosed between opening and closing tags, such as <name>John</name>. XML is very flexible and can be used to represent different types of information, such as documents, configuration data, or messages.

- **JSON** (*JavaScript Object Notation*):
  It uses a syntax based on key-value pairs to represent data. For example, "name": "John". JSON is widely used in the context of the web and JavaScript applications but can also be used in other contexts.

Macro Area: Data Security

- ***General Data Protection Regulation (GDPR):***
  The GDPR is a European regulation that establishes rules on the protection of personal data and the rights of individuals regarding the processing of such data.

- ***Personal Data:***
  Refers to information that identifies or can be used to identify an individual, such as name, address, phone number, email address, etc.

- ***Consent:***
  Consent is a freely given, specific, informed, and unambiguous indication of the data subject's wishes by which he or she agrees to the processing of personal data.

- ***Transparency:***
  Represents organizations' obligation to provide clear, complete, and understandable information about the processing of personal data, including the purposes for which the data is collected and how it will be used.

- ***Rights of Data Subjects:***
  Refers to the rights conferred to individuals by the GDPR, including the right to access their data, the right to rectification, the right to erasure, the right to restriction of processing, and the right to data portability.

- ***Data Protection Authority:***
  These are national authorities responsible for

enforcing the GDPR within each European Union Member State. They are responsible for ensuring compliance with data protection rules and sanctioning any violations.

- **Personal Data Breach**:
Represents a security incident that leads to the destruction, loss, alteration, unauthorized disclosure, or access to personal data.

- **Right to be Forgotten**:
Is an individual's right to request the erasure or removal of their personal data from an organization that has collected or is using it.

- **Privacy**:
Refers to an individual's right to maintain control over their personal information and decide how and when this information can be used or disclosed.

www.ingramcontent.com/pod-product-compliance
Lightning Source LLC
La Vergne TN
LVHW051739050326
832903LV00023B/1012